T0193832

O TO BE RIGHTEOUS

O TO BE RIGHTEOUS

Poems Along the Way

POEMS BY HUBERT MCMANUS

WESTBOW
PRESS®
A DIVISION OF THOMAS NELSON
& ZONDERVAN

WestBow Press books may be ordered through booksellers or by contacting:

WestBow Press
A Division of Thomas Nelson & Zondervan
1663 Liberty Drive
Bloomington, IN 47403
www.westbowpress.com
1 (866) 928-1240

ISBN: 978-1-9736-5756-9 (sc)
ISBN: 978-1-9736-5752-1 (e)

Library of Congress Control Number: 2019903387

Print information available on the last page.

WestBow Press rev. date: 4/4/2019

CONTENTS

A DOG TO HIS VOMIT

Like a dog to his vomit I return to my sin
And spit in the face of my Redeemer again
I cry out like Paul doing things that I hate
As I fail once again – O my sin is so great

Like a maggot filled carcass the stench of my pride
Screams I don't need You or the grace You provide
But I know in my heart it's Satan's lie being told
And that Messiah has come as the prophets foretold

What will it take to make me truly repent
To turn from my sin, my immoral descent
Why can't I turn, embrace His mercy so sweet
Leaving sin far behind, falling down at His feet

Jesus please help me; give the strength I so need
To flee from this sin with great vigor and speed
Shield my eyes from all evil, subdue unholy desires
Burn the dross of my sin in your unquenchable fire

How can You love me when I'm so out of control
Jesus, how could You save so disgusting a soul
How can Your grace extend to one such as me
Jesus, how can a just God set such a soul free

A just God demands there be payment for sin
I would have paid it had not Jesus stepped in
So thank you my Savior for bearing my pain
May this dog never turn to his vomit again

Your love is a mystery I can not comprehend
Yet Your Spirit within me testifies of Your plan
Continue to cleanse me until the day that I soar
To be home with Jesus and to sin never more

Sin's like a black hole in which there's no light
And grace like the sun that o'er powers the night
So thank you my Father though sin still lies within
The grace of my Savior is so much greater than sin

Hubert McManus
September 2004

A FUTURE THAT IS SURE

(Genesis 50:20, Romans 8:28)

What you meant for evil God has turned for my good
A mystery of life - embraced but not understood
Satan sends out arrows; God just turns them back
What is it we should fear of the Evil One's attack?

Satan sends out poison; but our God has the cure
Our protection is as certain as God's promises are sure
All the trials that beset us and cause us so much pain
Our omniscient God changes so only good will remain

Sovereign love expressed in God's one begotten Son
Guaranteed for our good -our victory's been won.
For His sovereign purpose for He is First and He is Last
My future now so certain that it can be spoken of as past.

Hubert McManus
October 28, 2004
(With thanks to Spink,
Alexander, Spurgeon, Calvin)

ANGER

(Ecclesiastes 7:9-10, Ephesians 4:31-32, Colossians 3:8)

My anger burns like some fire deep within
Consuming my peace – what a terrible sin.
Its temperature rises degree by degree
Erupting in passion – making a fool out of me.

Fueled by bitterness, malice and pride.
It spews forth like venom from deep down inside.
My flesh can't control it –does not even try
It's focus on me instead of God the Most High

It can't stay inside me – it must have release
Only Jesus can take it – replace it with peace.
His love alone can anger's rage quench
And remove from my life its vile, evil stench.

Hubert McManus
July 2001

CHOSEN BY GOD

(2 Thessolonians 2:13-14, John 6:4)

Chosen by God, how can it be,
That before time began He really chose me.
Chosen by God for nothing I've done,
Changed by His Spirit, Redeemed by His Son.

Chosen by God, what a sweet mystery,
Saved by the grace He poured out on me.
All for His glory before there was time,
Transferred to Jesus all the sins that were mine.

Drawn by the Father to the foot of the cross,
Reborn there I kneel and "count it all loss,"
Drawn to the Father out of my sin,
Washed by His blood without and within.

Chosen by God, how can it be,
That heaven is waiting for one such as me.
In heaven, my home, eternal praises I sing,
To Jesus my Savior, Redeemer, and King.

McManus

COME TO ME

(Matthew 11:28-30, John 6:35, 7:37, 14:27, Colossians
2:13-14, I Corinthians 1:26-31, II Corinthians 6:1-3)

Come to Me find perfect rest
Bring your fears, your pain, your stress
Come believe that you may live
Dwell within the peace I give

Come and drink – quench your thirst
Find in Me your life's new birth
Come and taste the Living Bread
Find life in Him who raised the dead

Come and bring your grief and pain
To the One who died but rose again
Come and all my fullness see
Confess, repent, leave sin with Me

Come thru the Door; know true peace
Bring all your pain and find release
Come be healed; find mercy here
Leave behind your angst and fear

Come to Me, My Son embrace
Find in Him your hiding place
Come and in My bosom hide
Safe within Our love reside

Come to Me you need not be wise
To find the faith Your God supplies
Come find hope and peace and joy
That man can't tarnish or destroy.

Come right now don't turn away
Receive new life- right now- today
Come know a love as yet unknown
Found only at your Savior's throne

Hubert McManus
February 2005

CRUSHED (ISAIAH 53)

Men were not drawn to Your suave, handsome face
Elegant trappings, even the appeal of Your grace
Despised and rejected full of sorrow and of grief
You were pierced, beaten, crushed for my unbelief

You were smitten by God – and afflicted for me
And for my sin punished, as you died on that tree
I, like my brothers, wandered so far, far astray
God punished You because I went my own way

God's will was to crush You, make You suffer and die
Make Your grave with the wicked so I might have life
Like a Lamb You were slaughtered because of my sin
Healed by Your wounds, You're my hope at life's end

You bear the sins of so many - not just for me all alone
It was for many transgressors Your blood did atone
Your death on the cross made my salvation complete
Yet You committed no wrong nor was in You deceit

Many made righteous because You suffered and died
Many have hope because Your blood's been applied
Many hearts have been cleansed by Your sacrifice
Many souls now in heaven because You gave them life.

Hubert McManus
June 2004

FACE TO FACE

Face to face I cannot wait
No more killing, pain, or hate
Face to face engulfed by Light
Always day - no more night

Face to face I lift my voice
Eternal praise for Sovereign choice
Face to face with the One who came
Took on Himself my sin and shame

Face to face with my Priest and King
My knees bow down, my praises ring
Face to face with my loving Friend
The One who died to become my sin

Face to face with the Prince of Peace
To Bow in awe in that Holy Place
Face to face there's no more fears
No more sickness, sorrow, tears

Face to face inhibitions gone
Bask in His love, break out in song
Face to face O how will it be
In Jesus' presence who died for me

Face to face my place prepared
Eternity now with my Jesus shared
Face to face I cannot comprehend
Eternal joy where praise does not end

Hubert McManus
February 2004

FATHER I COME

Father, I come just to sit on Your lap,
To feel Your strong arms as around me they wrap.
I have no request and I bring You no list;
My head on Your chest is just something I've missed.

I just want to listen, to really hear what You say;
To bask in Your love and, then, learn to obey.
You know all of my needs, all my hidden desires;
You know what to nourish; what to burn in the fire.

You know all my weakness, all my sin and distress;
You know what to curse and You know what to bless.
You know how I fail and see my frail, weary heart
Yet because You still love me; it won't keep us apart.

So I come to You Father, for the joy that it gives;
You know who I am and yet still You forgive;
Hold onto me Father with Your warm, sure embrace
My heart's bursting with thanks for the smile on Your face

Hubert McManus
February 27, 2008
Inspired by Larry Crabb's The
PAPA Prayer

GIVING

(Luke 6:38)

To give to someone without the means to repay
Comes from the Lord - for this is ever His way.
To give without thought of one's comfort or gain
Shows His church realizes why our Savior was slain
To give with true love and not give to impress
Will accrue to the giver God's promise to bless
Thanks Brother and Sister for sacrifices you've made;
May our faithful, true God see your kindness repaid

GLORIFIED

(Romans 8:18-29) work in progress

Our bodies ache; bone tired and sore
Awaiting the return of Jesus once more
O glorious day of our Savior's return
The Beast to defeat, shackle and burn

Creation groans as though giving birth
Awaiting the Messiah's return to this earth
O Christ return, our new bodies give
Your adopted take home in heaven to live

O glorious day when our suffering yields
To the glory promised, to hope that's fulfilled
In Christ we will stand; in Christ justified
We yearn for the day we will be glorified

Hubert McManus
October 26, 2004

GOD'S GOLDEN CHAIN

(Romans 8:29-30)

Paul gives to us a golden chain, forged by God above
A chain that can't be broken - formed from a heart of love
Shaped by grace and mercy - I scarce can understand
The priceless Gift extended, Who met the law's demand

My God He has **foreknown** me; 'twas His eternal plan
Ordained before the world was formed, by His almighty hand
He did not look and see my choice-a choice I could forsake
It was His choice and in His plan - this decision I would make

O glorious thought He **predestined** me long 'ere this world began
Elect in Christ and known by Him, my name written on His hand.
He predestined me by His own choice; O I cannot comprehend
Why He would pluck me from the fire and bid me call Him Friend

For nothing good was found in me; yet still He **called** me out.
Now I praise with every breath and sing and dance and shout.
I could not come until He called; I was hopeless, dead in sin
Until He gave me ears to hear and new life there within

I was a slave in sin's death grip, unrighteous and undone
Then Jesus came, died for me and made me with You one
Justified by Christ my God – something I could never do
Imputed now to me His life; He's made me one with You

I who was dead and had no hope, save hell's eternal flame,
Am reconciled in Christ to You, set free from guilt and shame.
Glorified – all sin removed- face to face with Christ my King
My knees will bow, arms will rise and lips Your praise will sing

Hubert McManus
April 26, 2004

GRACE OR WRATH?

**(Matthew 24:4-5, Ephesians 5:6, Colossians
3:6, Revelation 14:10 // Micah 7:18,
Colossians 2:14, I Peter 1:2-4)**

Oh the cup of God's wrath is filled to the brim
To be poured out one day if you reject Him,
If you find yourself trusting man's empty words
One day you will reap His just and holy reward

Will you drink wrath from the Almighty's cup,
Face eternal pain that won't ease or let up?
Did you know that God's anger is an eternal fire?
Is to suffer agony forever really what you desire?

Have you accepted the lies being told every day -
Sin won't be punished; there is no price to pay
There's not just One Way to God, all people must go
You can not reject Jesus and not be God's foe.

Please consider His wrath, understand He is just
Do not trust in things that will fade, burn and rust
Acknowledge your sin; turn to Jesus – God's Son
For without Him you're lost and forever undone.

Only His grace can cover your sin and your guilt
Only His love destroys strongholds you've built
He delights to show mercy, give you His peace
Wrapped in His arms all your turmoil will cease

The price was too high Jesus paid on the cross
To think that His love now could ever be lost
His sacrifice was perfectly spotless and pure
God's grace given forever, firm, true and sure

Jesus calls you, waiting - His arms open wide
The price fully paid-see His hands, see His side
He died for you – on the cross took your sin
Oh run to Him now, see your new life begin

Hubert McManus
July 2004

IF YOUR CHURCH
IS ALL WHITE

If your church is all white maybe your god is too small
Maybe tears ought to flow as to your knees you now fall
If your church is all white where are all your black friends?
Maybe it is time to repent before the Lord comes again

If your church is all white maybe your doctrine is wrong
Does it make God happy just to sing the right songs?
If your church is all white something's missing you see
One of our Savior's last prayers was for Church unity

If your church is all white there are questions to pose
To your segregated worship is He agreed or opposed?
If your church is all white you might want to pray
And then be still and listen to what God has to say

Hubert McManus
December 2007

LIFE IN THE SPIRIT

(Galatians 5)

We have been called-called to be free
Me serving you and you serving me
The way I love me I must also love you
The Law summed up in one word or two

Life in the Spirit expressing love, joy, peace
Hatred, discord, selfish ambition must cease
As patience, kindness, self-control take hold
Put off the envy, orgies and dissension of old

In step with the Spirit, faithful, gentle and kind
No impure thoughts, lust or by idols confined
Now living in Christ and with Him crucified
Declared righteous by God-in Christ justified

Hubert McManus
June 16, 2006

LIVING IN SIN

Can a man just continue living in sin
If the Spirit of God is living within?
Will Christ share His temple with evil each day
Won't His Spirit refuse to reside in this way?

If the same sin's committed time and again
What good is repentance and confession of sin?
Has repentance been made if a life has not changed
To believe that it has is sad, confusing and strange

When the Spirit convicts and the warning's ignored
When action follows temptation, sin's at the door
Expect that the Spirit will punish our intentional sin
He won't dwell with evil – just sit back and grin

When the flesh is too willing and lust runs too deep
And no effort is made His commandments to keep
Expect the fire of His wrath to consume and to burn
A hard lesson's coming – one that has to be learned

MADE IN YOUR IMAGE

(Genesis 1:1-27, Isaiah 46:9-11, 48:11, Romans 11:33-36,
Job 42:2, Acts 4:27-28, Luke 12:20, Ephesians 1:13-14)

You spoke and created by the force of Your words
All the mountains and flowers, all the oceans and birds
There is none other like You full of unfettered power
Timeless and ageless ten thousand years but an hour

Your wisdom is matchless; You're inscrutably wise
Your unfathomable presence fills earth, sea and skies
Your knowledge O God is incomprehensibly great
Your thoughts unknowable to this frail human state

You are righteous and holy and "Other" to man
Your vastness so great the world's in Your hand
A perfect, pure God in sovereign control
Not only of life but of every man's soul

Nothing escapes You – not one word or one thought
No contingency exists that can make You distraught
You see into my mind before a thought has been formed
Your providence controls both the prince and the storm

There is no god before You; You have no glory to share
At the ends of the earth I would still find You there
You are the Alpha, Omega; You have no beginning, no end
And though I look to the heavens even these You transcend

Yet I am made in Your image; how can such a thing be
You sent Your Only Begotten to save a worm such as me
O accept my thanks, Father, for the precious gift of Your Son
And for the work of salvation which Your Holy Spirit has done

Hubert McManus
August 29, 2004

MORNING PRAYER

(Psalm 5:3, Psalm 88:13, Psalm 92:2, Mark 1:35)

Each morning I rise to spend time with you
Longing again to be refreshed and renewed
Though the day is still dark – no light has yet shone
Your glory I see while on my knees at Your throne.

No sound to distract me from hearing Your voice
As I open Your Word and in Your precepts rejoice
How I covet this time when it is peaceful and still
Enveloped by silence Your Holy Presence I feel.

The new day is dawning and what joy fills my soul
To be wrapped in Your arms as the new day unfolds
Please hold back the sun for just a little while more
And let me bask in Your love-know unfettered rapport

I need a little more time here in the Spirit's embrace
More time with my Jesus – time to contemplate grace
Please hold off the sun – don't let the world enter in
How I yearn for that time when this feeling won't end

Hubert McManus
July 2004

MORNING THANKS
FOR CATHY

In the cool of the morning before there is light
Slowly I stroll - embrace what's left of the night
My thoughts turn to you as they do every day
I thank God for your love in the dark as I pray

Shared life together gives me purpose and worth
I know that for me there's only one person on earth
As moon turns to sunlight I watch it glisten on dew
And thank God for granting me life lived with you

Now home is in sight as the moon starts to fade
My prayer of thanksgiving's been joyfully made
God giving me you is a treasure precious and rare
So every day I thank Him for the love that we share

Hubert McManus
June 19, 2006

OH TO BE RIGHTEOUS

(Sing to the Tune: Blessed Assurance)

Oh to be righteous, just in Your sight,
Claim as did Paul to have fought the good fight,
A life that is holy, fleeing from sin,
Follow like Caleb, year out and year in.

Chorus:
This is my prayer, Lord, this is my plea:
To walk in a way that will glorify Thee.
This is my prayer, Lord, this is my plea:
To walk in a way that will glorify Thee.

O to be holy, ordained for Your use,
Confess as did David, no pause or excuse,
Honor and love You, with ne'er a restraint,
Fail as did Paul and still end up a saint. (Chorus)

Oh to be faithful in blessing or pain,
Obeying like Noah before any rain,
Trust You and serve You in darkness and light,
Stand before giants all clothed in Your might. (Chorus)

Oh to still know You, to understand grace
Like prophets before me to fall on my face,
Worship, adore You -- singing Your worth,
Like old Elijah taken from earth. (Chorus)

Oh to see Jesus, my Saviour and Lord,
Kissing the feet of the Glorified Word,
Thank Him forever for paying my debt,
Praise in a way I don't understand yet. (Chorus)

Hymn written by Riveroaks member, Hubert McManus, who initially submitted an original poem for the November 2001 Reflector. The poem was slightly modified and a chorus was added in order to set it to music.

POEM FOR MY BROTHER

All the tiny fish tremble at the very sound of his name
When the big 'uns get off there's always something to blame
But one has to admire Bill's relentless pursuit
Of a trophy to hang and a horn he can toot

But give Bill some credit 'cause he's tried them all
No species is safe from the empty space on his wall
Beware bass, bream and crappie-watch out salmon and trout
He is hot on your trail and your future's in doubt

But there is oh so much more to this story you see
'Cause when Bill goes afishin' its most time on his knees
He sure loves to catch fish of all shapes, weight and size
But man's eternal soul is his most coveted prize

So he studies God's Word and then proclaims it to man
And seeks the help of God's Spirit so that they'll understand
That there's but One Way to God – else
they're lost and hellbound
And he longs for them to seek Jesus
while He still can be found

Good luck with your fishin' Bill, my Brother and friend
I hope a big fish to that spot on your wall will ascend
Ahh but even more Bill, I pray that our God He will bless
Your ministry down here with much soul saving success!

I Love You Brother!

Hubert "Mac" McManus
August 2004

PRAYER

Father please forgive for the way that I pray
Taking no time to listen for what You have to say
O Abba forgive the wrong approach that I take
Not praying all day is such a terrible mistake

How can I approach You with almost no thought
Or thanks for salvation and how it was bought
I bring so little praise of Your mercy and grace
I fall on my pillow instead of my knees or my face

Father forgive that I do not schedule my day
To make time for You or to bow down and pray
I let the concerns of this life control what I do
I ignore Your instructions to give my troubles to You!

Father forgive me for hauling burdens around
When there at the cross true peace can be found
When all I need do to find comfort – relief
Is nail to the cross all my sin, pain and grief.

Surrounded by darkness I'm afraid in the night
When the Spirit is ready to supply me with light
I know that all I must do is bend down my knee
I know Jesus will listen - I have His Guarantee

Father please change me; do not leave me this way
Make communion with You the best part of my day
O Father please show me - there's nothing I can do
That even comes close to the time spent with You

Can I keep a promise when I've not made a vow?
Can I hear Jesus whisper if I'm not listening now?
O Father please fill me with sweet comfort and joy
Daily communion with You that can't be destroyed

Hubert McManus
November 2004

PRAYERS WITHOUT PASSION

Prayers without passion are just words that we say
A hunger for God should stir our souls when we pray
Prayers without boldness reveal a faith that is small
So trust in His promise that He's there when we call

Prayers without worship show just how little we know
Of a just, holy God who sees that we reap what we sow
Prayers without reverence declare we don't understand
An omnipotent God who holds all of life in His hand

Prayers without love are just a waste of our time
He knows all in our heart and looks into our mind
Prayers with out faith come from a cold, empty heart
A heart that needs Jesus and what His Spirit imparts

But when Jesus is King and His Spirit holds sway
In confidence we kneel, our God hears when we pray
With urgent petitions made with assurance and zeal
With passion and warmth we can share all we feel

For our Father says boldly let our petitions be known
So like a child to his father let us race to the throne
He is anxious to listen to every word we confide
We will find Him there waiting with arms open wide

Hubert McManus
Aug 23, 2004

PSALM 51

O just, holy Father all my sin you must hate.
Forgive me O God for Your mercy is great.
O wash me my God and cleanse me of sin
Purge from my life this false heart within.

Against You, You only I have sinned in Your sight.
So your judgment is just and my punishment right.
You delight when truth sinks deep roots in a man;
And Your Spirit sees fruit as he trusts in Your plan

O purge me with hyssop; then I will be clean.
In a clean heart O God Your Son can be seen.
O cast me not out, take not Your Spirit away
Restore all my joy; I'll show others the Way

For in sacrifice and offerings You find no delight -
But in a spirit that's broken and a heart that's contrite,
My lips must now praise Your eternal, good Name -
So that sinners see Jesus as Your love I proclaim.

RAINDROPS UNITED

(Psalm 133, John 17, Romans 15:5-7, Revelation 7:9-10)

When just one raindrop falls to the ground
Its goes unnoticed and makes 'nary a sound
But joined to its brothers puddles will form
And then run to the river from out of a storm

The river swells until it becomes a great flood
For miles solid ground will turn into mud
Drop joining drop until it fills up the sea -
A valuable lesson for those not to blind to see

One single raindrop has little power or force
Same's true for us if Satan keeps us divorced
Standing alone we're unimportant and weak
United in Christ we become something unique

When we all come together to worship the Son
Black man-white man praising God Three-in-One
Black joined to white the world cannot ignore
Such a display of God's love not seen here before

Why let the Father of Lies separate and deceive?
Segregated in worship the Holy Spirit we grieve.
Why not worship together as in heaven t'will be?
Showing God changes hearts of even bigots like me

Our Jesus He prayed we'd be all perfectly one
Each loving the other as the Father the Son
He ordained it this way so a lost world would know
That God sent the Son sovereign grace to bestow

Hubert McManus
March 2005

SNOWFLAKES

(John 17)

All Mine are Yours, and Yours are Mine too
I guarded them Father; I gave them to You
Unite them now Father make them all one
Join them in love for the sake of Your Son.

A single snowflake just floats in the air
And all by itself we don't know its there
But united with others a power is found
If enough join together a city shuts down

Why is our worship with just "our own kind"
Foregoing the power of sharing One mind
Do our ears just not hear our God when He calls
Or is the "god" that we serve simply too small.

In their love for each other My love will show
In this way alone the whole world will know
Just why You sent Me-what love truly means
When they're united in love Your glory is seen

Hubert McManus
October 2004

SPIRIT

(Mark 15:38, Gal 4:6, John 14:26,
1 Cor. 2:10, Eph. 5:15-21)

May I walk in Your Spirit LORD, please show me how
To let Your power reign in me; cast sin out right now
In my flesh I'm defeated; I am so lost and undone
Unless the power of Your Spirit shows me Your Son

You called me, changed me, helped me understand grace
Your Spirit's within me - not in some cold granite place
What joy, peace and comfort is now mine day to day
With no veil between us as I bow down and pray

Holy Spirit shine brightly where my dark secrets lie
All revealing, nothing's hidden as Your all-seeing eye
Examines my motives, exposing my sinful desires
Burns the dross of my sin in Your fierce, holy fires

O Spirit illumine, impart God's Word to me
There I'll see Jesus - how His cross sets me free
There I'll find mercy and what love really means
For in Jesus alone can Your Love truly be seen

Holy Spirit, my strength, my peace and joy every day
As You proclaim the Truth – "There is only One Way"
Only One Way to reach You, One Way I can trust
For my soul to find heaven as I return to the dust

Thanks be to You Father – You did not leave me alone
When my Savior returned to His place by Your throne
And thanks be for the change He has wrought in my heart
And for the eternal blessing His work of salvation imparts

Hubert McManus
June 2004

STRENGTH FOR THE BATTLE

Galatians 5: 16-24

O God of all mercy please pardon me
Give light to my eyes so that I may see
My Savior's face - in His bosom find rest
Repentance grant as my sin is confessed

Transform my heart – purge wicked ways
Grant fruit from the Spirit the rest of my days
In step with Your Spirit and no longer a fool
Your Spirit in me to cleanse, teach, and rule

Give me strength for the war raging within
Flesh fighting Spirit – the temptation to sin
The power of Your Spirit giving me hope
Holding to me on the steep slippery slope

'Til the loud trumpet blasts; I am called home
And prostrated I bow in awe at Your throne
Forever with Jesus and at last face to face
I behold all His glory and bask in His grace

TEACH ME TO PRAY

(Listening)

Teach me to pray, how to listen and hear
The sound as Your voice calms all my fear
Teach me to pray by not speaking at all
Waiting on You so I hear when You call

Teach me to pray and learn to silently wait
On Your Spirit to speak as I just meditate
Teach me to pray without making a sound
Reverently silent, bowed low to the ground

Teach me to pray, hushed, humbled, alone
Seeking Your face, prostrate at Your throne
Teach me to pray - in secret - silent and still
I long for Your Spirit my whole heart to fill

Teach me to pray – meek, broken and mute
Desire to know Jesus my life's chief pursuit
Teach me to pray in quiet assurance of grace
Safe there in the arms of my Savior's embrace

Hubert McManus
March 2005

THE CROSS
(SATISFACTION, SACRIFICE, SUBSTITUTION)

(Romans 3:25, 1 John 2:2, & 4:10, Hebrews
10:20-28, Isaiah 53:5, 11, I Peter 2:24, 3:18)

I have a debt which I can never repay
Left in my sin God will collect it one day
My sinful life God could not ignore
His wrath I should face forevermore

God's justice demands full payment be made
His elect receive mercy because Jesus has paid
The debt that they owed by a blood sacrifice.
Assuaging God's wrath – Christ's blood did suffice

The Son loved by God was cursed for my sin
Became my substitute, my punishment's end
Condescended to come, keep each word of the law
To be forsaken by God though with no defect or flaw

I must humbly consider the cross of my King
He satisfied my debt - I had nothing to bring
Atonement He made just as justice required
He took my place and the pain of Hell's fire

At the cross Jesus suffered God's wrath for me.
There He made payment and there set me free.
And now I do knell – bought, humbled, amazed,
My hope's in His love as I now sing His praise.

Hubert McManus
February 2005

THE WAY OUT OF SIN

(James 3:1-12, 1 Corinth 10:13)

You tell me to flee; instead I just wallow in sin
Give in to temptation, and I disobey once again
You warn me my tongue is evil, restless, untamed
It spews forth poison, uncontrolled, unrestrained

All temptation encountered is common to man
God gives the way out when I live by His plan
So why do I fail to use the resources He gives
His Word, Holy Spirit, the Son who yet lives

O please help me my God learn how to flee
To find the way out You've provided to me
To pray in the Spirit, to live by Your Word
Love Jesus more than the sin once preferred

Hubert McManus
January 18, 2006

THERE COMES A DAY

(2 Corinthians 5:1-10, Hebrews 4:3, Revelation21,
John 14:1-3, Revelation 7:16-18)

There comes a day when I can rest
All cares depart there on His breast
There comes a day when I will run
Into the arms of God's own Son

There comes a day tears will leave
When broken hearts no longer grieve
There comes a day when pain departs
Wrapped in His arms I know His heart

There comes a day no need of light
God's own glory o'er whelms the night
There comes a day all sin is gone
There at His feet beholding His throne

There comes a day when I will see
That place prepared by my Jesus for me
There comes a day I'll see His face
And know true peace in His loving embrace

There comes a day life's journey's past
This earthly shell's transformed at last
O come sweet day O trumpet blow
The sky's rolled back and home I go!

Hubert McManus
November 2, 2004

THE THRONE OF GRACE

(Romans 8:26-27, Hebrew 4:16)

The day is so dark; the night is so long
And Your grace seems so far, far away
But I am refreshed - begin to feel strong
When I fall to my knees and I pray

Heartbreak and burdens cling to my soul
Satan tells me I've nowhere to turn
Then Your Spirit steps in taking control
Uttering prayers that cannot be spurned

As I open Your Word - comfort it brings
And it calms all my doubts and my fears
It reminds me again I have the ear of the King
And there in His presence there's no reason for tears

Whenever I bow, even as You command
And at the cross all my burdens lay down
Against whatever comes with You I can stand
For there at Your throne peace and power are found

Hubert McManus
January 6, 2005

TWO HEARTS – TWENTY YEARS – FOR CATHY

Two hearts in rhythm beat perfectly as one
In love with each other, in love with the Son
Two hearts together through the struggles of life
Sharing heartbreak and joy as husband and wife.

Two hearts look to Jesus for strength that they need
Knowing He is the answer as to the Father they plead
Two hearts bound in love face the battle each day
Advance on their knees down the straight narrow way.

Two hearts richly blessed by their Father above
Have been given each other to cherish and love
Two hearts trusting Jesus when all else has failed
Cling to the cross where their sins have been nailed.

Two hearts filled with joy because of Jesus their King
They bow down before Him and their tribute they bring
Two hearts offer thanks for the gift freely given -
Eternity together with their Savior up in heaven.

With all my love,
Hubert
March 2004

After thought:
A Proverbs 31 woman given to a sinful man
And bound to him forever in God's eternal plan.
May I love you as completely as does Jesus His bride
It's the only way to thank Him for all I'm feeling inside

WHERE ARE THE NINE?

(Luke 17:12)

Ten of them stood at a distance that day
Abandoned and sick - forced to stay far away
They had learned of a Rabbi with a power so real
With a word or a touch any disease He could heal

They saw Him and hope just swelled up inside
"Master have mercy " each one of them cried.
Each of them knew control was out of their hands
Then Jesus turned and gave a simple command.

"Go to the priest" as required by God's law
And show that your flesh now has no flaw.
In faith each one turned to do just as He'd said
Be inspected, set free – the law's shackles to shed.

As they turned and obeyed healing took place
Nine kept on going - one turned, fell on his face
Yes only one paused - humbly offering up praise
Now freed from the pain suffered days upon days.

More astonishing still is this embarrassing fact;
It wasn't even a Jew who turned and came back.
The one praising so loudly for a plea not ignored
Was a Samaritan dog at the feet of the LORD!

Were the Jews ungrateful or too self-center to bring
Praise and thanksgiving for this gift from their King
They believed in His power and obeyed His command
But the right response to His grace did not comprehend.

Ten sought to be cured. Ten were made well.
Yet nine left our LORD still spiritually frail.
How like them I am as I pass through each day
Not acknowledging His blessings as I go on my way.

For just like the lepers I was hopeless, outcast
Consumed by my sin, overwhelmed by my past
Please Jesus forgive me I am just like the nine
Neglecting to thank You for to much of the time.

O Father be pleased as this offering I bring
As I fall on my knees and bow to my King
Giving thanks to my Jesus my Healer my Friend
May I never be counted with the nine once again.

WHY WORRY

(Matthew 6:25-34, 1 Peter 5:7, Psalm 56:3, Is 41:8-10)

This world is filled with anxious fears
Despairing lives, pain, trouble, tears.
I wring my hands and pace and cry
And my lack of faith's the reason why.

Restless hearts yield sleepless nights
Burdened minds don't see things right
Consuming cares suck joy from life
When one's focus is not fixed on Christ

Our sin and grief – all our worldly woes
Come crashing down like a tyrant's blows
They beat and batter; they break and burn
Our faith attacked no matter where we turn

But our Savior said that our Father knows
Our every need for both food and clothes
He tenderly cares for the flower and bird
His provision as sure as His holy word

Seek first His kingdom O foolish child
Don't live in fear, deceived, beguiled
Heartaches and fear will become a hymn
As the burden's passed from you to Him

Hubert McManus
March 16, 2006

YOU ARE:

Light in the darkness; sight to the blind
Peace in the storm; good, merciful, kind
The Living Water to all those who thirst
Hope to the blessed, wrath to the cursed.

Man's only hope, if called always there
The giver of life, Intercessor in prayer
Transcendent beauty, jealous and feared
Calm in the storm, the One always near

Rest to the weary, Savior, Master and King
The salvation of many, the reason we sing
Bread for the hungry, worthy of praise
Bright Morning Star, the Ancient of Days

The true Root of David, Branch of the Lord
Hope of the gentile, the holy incarnate Word
Our Counselor, Comforter, our Emmanuel
The God-man who among mortals did dwell

Glorious Messiah, the Life, Truth and Way
Lamb sent from God who takes sin away
Alpha, Omega the Beginning and End
The Only Begotten and my truest Friend

Bridegroom, Creator, Light of the World
Prophet and Priest, God's Banner unfurled
The Rock of All Ages, Gate for the Sheep
Desire of the Nations who makes my heart leap

The Author of Faith, the Redeemer of man
The Finisher of Faith even before life began
Everlasting Father, the Lord of all lords
King of all kings who cannot be ignored

Blessed Redeemer, God's Beloved Son,
Head of the Church, God Three in One
Consolation of Israel, God's own AMEN
The First and the Last, Salvation from Sin

Hubert McManus

JESUS CARES

Bullets fly
Children die
Empty stares
No one cares

Nighttime falls
Hungry squalls
Empty stares
No one cares

Needles-n-arms
No one alarmed
Empty stares
No one cares

Kids with no dad
So bitter and sad
Empty stares
No one cares

Young girl raped
No way of escape
Empty stares
No one cares

Money's all gone
All help withdrawn
Empty stares
No one cares

Child cannot speak
Malnourished and weak
Empty stares
No one cares

Widows who cry,
Grow tired, old and die
Empty stares
No one cares

In God's own elect
Is there guilt & neglect?
In His house empty stares
Proclaim no one there cares?

If God's people meet
Without washing feet
With just empty stares
Does anyone care?

It's faith without works
If compassion is shirked.
Do our cold, empty stares
Say no one really cares?

Grace without love
Can't be from above
When cold, empty stares
Say no one really cares.

A cruel cross prepared
His Son was not spared
But eternity shared
Our Jesus cared!

Printed in the United States
By Bookmasters